A LIFE IN THIRTY-FIVE BOXES

ALSO BY DAVE HASLAM

Manchester, England: The Story of the Pop Cult City
Adventures on the Wheels of Steel: The Rise of the Superstar DJs
Not Abba: The Real Story of the 1970s
Life After Dark: A History of British Nightclubs & Music Venues
Sonic Youth Slept On My Floor: Music, Manchester, and More

A LIFE IN THIRTY-FIVE BOXES

How I Survived Selling My Record Collection

DAVE HASLAM

First published in the UK by Cōnfingō Publishing, 2019

249 Burton Road, Didsbury, Manchester, M20 2WA
www.confingopublishing.uk

Design & Typesetting by Zoë McLean, zoe@confingopublishing.uk

Printed and bound by TJ International Ltd

A CIP catalogue record for this book is available from the British Library

ISBN 978-0-9955966-3-4

2 4 6 8 10 9 7 5 3 1

To KT and Guy, with love.

The motives and joys of vinyl collectors are no doubt shared by anyone who chases down objects, and artefacts of any sort, to build a collection.

There doesn't seem to be much that someone somewhere doesn't deem reasonable to collect; for example, shoes, beer mats, pebbles from the beach, vintage cameras even if they don't work, anything pig-related, fridge magnets, African figurines, cashmere sweaters.

I wonder: do we have a compulsion to collect? Some of my friends and relations have big collections of books, and magazines; they're not pathological hoarders, or even consciously collecting, they just don't want to throw things away. Few of us own only a few possessions. We hold on to things, even when we don't really know why. If you don't throw things away, you're collecting; by default.

Why do so many of us hug pieces of vinyl to our hearts? Because we know that each record is so much more than a hundred and twenty grams of treated and pressed polyvinyl chloride resin. Each record is a tangible token of who we were when we fell in love with that piece of music. The collection, however small and disorganised, represents a personal journey through music, our changing passions, our pleasures, our life. Our moments of rapture, our moments of regret.

It used to be said of James Joyce – including by the man himself – that if Dublin were destroyed, it could be rebuilt in its entirety from the contents of his short stories and novels. Perhaps a person's music library has a similar power; that our life story could be reconstituted from the records we own.

I could have told you where I bought every piece of vinyl, and where I was when I first heard every piece of music, and where I was living when the record was added to the collection and where I was DJ'ing, but, despite all that history, and my attachment to the tunes, in September 2015 I decided to sell all my vinyl.

I put four and a half thousand pieces on sale; the complete collection, including records I'd bought forty years earlier, and many I'd played DJ'ing in the Haçienda in Manchester and other clubs and venues. I loved those kilos of chloride resin, but, at the same time, I realised I was ready to let go.

Over the following pages we'll hear of people with significant collections of vinyl. We'll discuss the pleasures and perils of collecting, and recall trips to record shops, great finds, favourite tunes. I'll explain and track how my collection grew, but then ended up parcel-taped into thirty-five boxes and driven away from my house in a large white van.

+

Some people may have a stronger innate propensity to collect. Do we derive deep-seated comfort and security from surrounding ourselves with familiar and loved objects? We're deepening a passion with a collection; although, for some, I know that trading stuff is as much a part of the thrill as possessing it.

Collectors enjoy the chase. Some record collectors pursue a very focused hunt; they have a wants list, and search for specific releases. They're motivated by an urge to find a rarity, or to complete a set. Other record collectors are led less by a list, and more by natural instinct. Theirs is a random hunt, crate-digging in record stores, checking the bargain bins, trawling secondhand or charity shops. They'll find a record, take a gamble on it and make a spontaneous purchase.

The impulse to collect hits many of us at an early age, when our heads are turned by toy dinosaurs maybe, or dolls, and/or Panini stickers. Ex-fanzine editor Dec Hickey has a collector's mentality which goes back years: 'I genuinely feel my collecting obsession can be traced back to the cards and books PG Tips regularly knocked out in the sixties.'

Tea manufacturers PG Tips were one of many companies throughout the twentieth century which took advantage of our collecting impulse to ramp up demand for their product. A hundred years ago, tobacco company Wills would include a small card with a photograph or illustration on a set theme in each pack of cigarettes. If the smoker wasn't a collector, a family member often was. When they were young, my grandparents collected cigarette cards. My grandmother had books full of complete sets of actors and actresses, and of flowers. My grandfather collected cricketers.

Dec recalls a particular interest: 'I remember getting heavily into butterflies, and waiting for Mum to come back from the shops so I could open the PG Tips packet and grab the cards.'

Dec and I corresponded and met a couple of

times in the 1980s, our music tastes coinciding – bands like New Order, Cabaret Voltaire. His passion for New Order grew; he documented and photographed gigs, and collected cassette recordings of live shows.

On one occasion around 1985 Dec surprised me by name-checking José Feliciano – a Puerto Rican vocalist and guitarist a world away from the weird electro/industrial stuff that I was used to Dec talking to me about. I'd only heard his cover version of 'Light My Fire' from 1968 but Dec knew everything he'd released. Many years later, he is still a Feliciano fan, a collector and a completist – to an astonishing degree.

He recently explained to me that he has a spreadsheet of every José Feliciano 7" single he either has or is aware of. Many of them are the same song, but released in different countries. Currently his spreadsheet lists 1,403 different pressings, covering 46 countries. When the singles regularly arrive, from Japan, or Mexico, or wherever, he doesn't play them. 'I don't need to,' he says. 'I've heard the songs a thousand times. I tick them off the list, and file them away.'

You need to collect the set?

'Yes, I do. It's laughable really, but it is the collecting-the-set thing, or at least trying to.'

Fifty years on from hoping for a picture of a red admiral, Dec gets his kicks from going on the net and finding copies of Feliciano's 'Light My Fire' he didn't know existed. 'I have ten different pressings of José's "Light My Fire" UK RCA 7", he tells me. 'All with very slightly different labels.'

He knows I'm a bit stunned by this information.

'Yes, I converse with other Feliciano collectors and we laugh about the madness of it all.'

One of the pleasures of being human can be the interactions with others who follow the same interest. The world of collectors has some of this fellowship and camaraderie, although there can be an underlying sense of competition too, and a degree of tension in the group, especially if there's a search for the same holy grail, the same rarities.

Some collecting is necessary, and practical. My sister lives in the Shropshire countryside and spends the autumn building up a store of wood to feed the fire that keeps her warm in winter. Her annual ritual of collecting wood connects her to a seasonal, human activity that's been taking place for thousands of years.

For decades, there was a practical reason to buy records. You could catch music live, or find a decent DJ on a radio station or in a club, but if you wanted to listen to the music of your choice, there wasn't a viable alternative to owning an artefact: the disc.

You can guess that some collections began for practical reasons, but then tipped over into something obsessive. My friend Keith collects trainers. He has over a hundred and fifty pairs. How many is a practical solution to everyday footwear issues? And when does buying trainers become an obsession?

Most people collect items that appear to have no practical benefit. Bass-player Mani has a Toby jug collection.[1] It's an eccentric choice: what use or value do they have? But then does it even matter what value they have? If collecting – whatever, whenever – helps to push a person one rung up the ladder of happiness, it's invaluable. As film-maker Wim Wenders once remarked, 'My advice is don't spend your money on therapy. Spend it in a record store.'

Actress Claudia Schiffer is an insect enthusiast. You'd think that – like most of the population – she'd shy away from creepy-crawlies, but if she had a fear, she's conquered it. Her houses are filled with insect art, and her collections of pinned and mounted butterflies, moths and spiders.[2] 'As a child,' she once

---

[1] Gary 'Mani' Mounfield, bass-player in the Stone Roses and Primal Scream.
[2] *Daily Telegraph*, 27 July 2011.

explained, 'I was fascinated with spiders' webs spar-
kling with morning dew, or just after the rain.'

+

In eras when the only available format was a physical object – not a WAV or an MP3 – it was, at worst,
unavoidable, or, at best, part of a wonderful ritual,
that gaining access to your favourite music entailed
visiting a record shop.

 Records were possibly one of the first things
you bought with your own saved-up pocket money or
a Christmas gift token. So, in many ways, the process
of buying records came with a sense of freedom, of
growing up, of becoming your own person.

 Our early experiences of music-buying coin-
cide with our most porous years, those years of our
youth when we're beginning to absorb what's around
us and settle into who we are and look for a place in
the world. Our musical tastes are connected with our
sense of identity. Our purchases reflect who we are but
also who we want to be.

 On a Sunday my parents liked to go to church,
and to take their three kids with them (I was the
well-adjusted middle child). We often required a little cajoling, it has to be said. But there were occasions
when I was a willing churchgoer: on the Sundays I'd

saved enough pocket money to go buy a record after the service.

Over the road from the church there was a newsagent which sold 7" singles. The selection was limited to songs in the charts, or hovering around them. They were displayed on a rotating wire stand, just stuffed in there haphazardly, untidily. The shop had a bigger selection of greetings cards than records.

I imagine that through most of 1972 'My Ding-a-Ling' by Chuck Berry would have been on sale there – you would expect to pay 35p for that – or 'All the Young Dudes' by Mott the Hoople. That was how much I paid there for my first-ever vinyl purchase – the single 'Telegram Sam' by T-Rex.

I guess it's appropriate that from my youngest days record-buying was associated with trips to church. Music became like a religion to me. By the end of the 1970s, I'd come to revere Debbie Harry and Siouxsie Sioux; Iggy Pop would be my patron saint; and I'd worship Joy Division.

Soon I began to frequent record shops that were a lot more specialist than my neighbourhood newsagent. In those early days I marvelled at the magical properties of the bits of 35p plastic. I'd hold the record delicately in my hands, turning it over, each record a sacred object. And I'm not sure I ever quite lost that.

Years later, 1989 or so, I'd leave Eastern Bloc on Oldham Street, Manchester, having purchased there some import 12" single released by an undercapital-ised label in Detroit or New York, one of a thousand records pressed maybe – a hundred had arrived in the UK, perhaps twenty were stocked in Manchester record shops, of which ten were in Eastern Bloc – and I had one of them. It had made a long journey to meet me, and I couldn't wait to play it that weekend at the Haçienda. I'd take the record home with just the same excitement I'd once felt clutching 'Telegram Sam'.

Most of the pop music my older sister and my younger brother and I were exposed to were songs on the TV show *Top of the Pop*s and daytime BBC Radio One. Our parents had three children under five years old in 1963 – hardly conducive to throwing them-selves into the Swinging Sixties. Pop music wasn't their thing but they had a few dozen classical records, including *Pictures at an Exhibition* by Russian com-poser Mussorgsky, which I adored.

Among my sister's first vinyl purchases were 7" singles by Rod Stewart, including 'Stay With Me' and 'Maggie May', and his album *Never a Dull Moment*. When she joined a youth club, she began discover-ing music beyond the charts. She started buying and bringing home Bob Dylan, Neil Young and Fairport Convention albums.

In the mid 1970s you couldn't escape the sense that my generation was coming into adulthood in the wake of a golden age. That whatever happened in our era, nothing would compare to the great explosion of creativity, youth culture, and radical politics in the 1960s. By the time my teenage years began, Jimi Hendrix was dead, flower power had wilted, and the Beatles had broken up.

I went back in time for most of my first album purchases, including a couple of Jimi Hendrix albums: the *Smash Hits* album – a compilation (cheap, as compilations tend to be) – and a copy of *Electric Ladyland* (the version released on Reprise that was packaged without the salacious photo on the Track release but that included 'All Along the Watchtower').

I didn't have to own every album I wanted to listen to. One of the lads next door had a much bigger Black Sabbath collection than me. If I wanted to listen to 'War Pigs', I'd go round there. In addition, my sister's friends would sometimes lend me music; I'm still scratching my head about the Wishbone Ash album *Argus* which an older lad let me borrow from him for a week.

Albums weren't on sale at the newsagent, so

LP record-buying required a trip into town. Shops like
The Diskery on Bromsgrove Street and Reddington's
Rare Records near the Bull Ring sold me some of rock
and roll history's early touchstones, including John
Lee Hooker albums from 1959 and 1960. And records
from a less distant past, like *Disraeli Gears* and *Wheels
of Fire* by Cream (released 1967 and 1968 respec-
tively). The psychedelic cover designs by Martin
Sharp on both the Cream albums fascinated me but,
in the end, the records were a big disappointment –
apart from the sleeves, and 'Tales of Brave Ulysses'.

By 1977 I was more interested in newer music
than losing myself in the past. This was thanks to dis-
covering *New Musical Express* (*NME*) and John Peel. It
was hearing 'The Passenger' on John Peel that turned
me on to Iggy Pop; the fifteen-year-old me loved the
sense of adventure and possibility in the lyric. Iggy's
Lust For Life was the first album I bought from the
local HMV store, which became the place where I
most often shopped for contemporary albums (I went
to Inferno for singles).

There were many big-hitting rock acts
(Fleetwood Mac's and ELO's albums were huge in
1978), but also punk and new wave were winning
new converts, and disco music was at its commercial height. 1978 was the biggest year ever for sales of

singles in the UK. In addition, there were 86 million album sales in the UK that year, nearly 1.5 million of which were the *Saturday Night Fever* soundtrack.

Sales of vinyl albums declined through the 1980s, after the compact disc format was introduced; by 1994 they had dropped to 1.5 per cent as compact discs (CDs) took over.[3] At the beginning of the 2000s, illegal and legal downloads were all-conquering, and vinyl sales were dwindling.

It's well known that vinyl sales have increased in recent years, with a turning point around 2011.[4] Numerous Manchester shops, including Piccadilly Records and Eastern Bloc, are doing great business, Spillers in Cardiff (founded in 1894, and reputed to be the oldest record shop in the world) is thriving, and Reckless Records in Soho recently expanded its premises. In recent months I've visited a number of great little vinyl stores, including the Record Café in Bradford, and Strand in Stoke (both have a good stock of tunes, but also act as social hubs – as the best record shops often are).

The revival of vinyl is a cause for much rejoic-

---

[3] *The Economist*, 18 May 2017.
[4] Adam Teskey, manufacturing director at The Vinyl Factory, talking to Ben Wardle, https://www.longlivevinyl.net/pressing-concerns-the-new-breed-of-vinyl-pressing-plant (consulted January 2019).

ing but here's some context: the British Phonographic Industry (BPI) reported 4.2 million album sales in 2018, the highest figure since the early nineties but less than 5 per cent of the total number of albums sold in this country in 1978.[5]

At this time, the *NME* was probably the strongest influence on my record purchases. In 1980 I read a review of a single by a band called Deutsch Amerikanische Freundschaft. The single was 'Kebabträume'. I hadn't heard the record but I was inspired enough by whatever the hundred words said to get the bus to town.

Imagine getting to the counter at Inferno and asking the fella there if he has a copy of 'Kebabträume' by Deutsch Amerikanische Freundschaft? I was a teenager, I was nervous, social interactions weren't stress-free. For the song title and the name of the band I put on a German accent, which I'd got from watching the TV series *Colditz*.

After four attempts, the guy asked me to say the band's name yet again.

'Ah, daff!' he exclaimed.

They were calling themselves DAF (pro-

[5] https://www.musicbusinessworldwide.com/uk-record-industry-enjoys-109m-annual-growth-but-album-sales-tanked-in-2018 (consulted January 2019).

nounced 'daff'). I bought the 7" for 65p. It's now worth a tenner.

I guess my tastes were for what we now call 'post-punk'. But, at the same time, I felt inspired and able to cross the tribes, even from punk to disco. In *Sonic Youth Slept On My Floor*, I write about the moment I left a Generation X concert early and fell in love with 'Can You Feel the Force?' by the Real Thing. At home I had a foster brother called Richard who'd disappear on Saturday or Sunday afternoons to attend jazz-funk all-dayers. At school, a girl did an end-of-term dance routine to 'Now That We've Found Love' by Third World.

This was the end of the 1970s, an era of music tribalism; the punks fought the body-poppers, the skins fought the mods, the soul boys hated the long hairs. I couldn't quite see the point of fearing each other, or fighting over our music tastes, while Thatcher was enacting policies that were sending youth unemployment sky-high, and I didn't want to limit myself as a music lover either. In any case, John Peel was pushing my tastes in an eclectic direction, introducing me to bands like the Pop Group and the Specials.

I wasn't a purist, I wasn't wedded to the idea of obsessing over touchstones from the past. I wanted music that spoke of the now, and something that crossed over boundaries, broke rules. Something like the paranoid punk angst, soul, passion, punch, emotion, poetry, and politics of the first Dexys Midnight Runners album, *Searching for the Young Soul Rebels*, which, thanks to HMV, took pride of place in my collection on the day of its release in July 1980.

+

Neurologist Oliver Sacks once wrote that music evokes 'remembered worlds of events, people, places we have known'.[6] Unbidden, a tune might bring back the memory of a youth club disco; a particular night out; a record that comforted us during a period in which we were floundering; a person who we wish was still in our life; a face, a place, an emotion.

I hear something from the first Electribe 101 album and I'm in my late twenties again, awash with the pleasures and uncertainties of being a new dad. I hear 'Rockit' by Herbie Hancock and I'm transported to Hulme, it's the summer of 1983 and that record seems to be blaring from every open window from Duxbury Square all the way over to the Crescents. Play me Tapper Zukie's 'MPLA' and I'm at Barbarella's in 1978 and the punks are dancing.

---

[6] Oliver Sacks, *Musicophilia: Tales of Music and the Brain* (Knopf, 2007).

A collection reminds us of the road we've travelled and provides a link back to our past. Cultural historian Mihaly Csikszentmihalyi identifies 'continuity of self' as an important element in why we hold on to, and collect, things.[7] Maybe you don't even need to hear the vinyl; you can grab that gatefold sleeve, the battered 12", the picture disc 7", and surf a time machine back to good times, odd times, or the best times.

Like a collection of any kind, my records were my pride and joy. Some of them I'd had with me for forty years, including the records I packed when I moved from Birmingham to Manchester. Some records in the collection I bought when I was a student mooching around record shops such as Piccadilly Records, HMV on Market Street, Robinson's Records on Blackfriars Street, and Yanks on Chepstow Street.

I carried my boxes of records from student accommodation near Whitworth Park to a succession of homes in Longsight, Hulme, Whalley Range, and Moss Side. I was all over the place, literally and metaphorically. I was running a fanzine, putting on bands, and had a cheap office in a room in an old warehouse

---

[7] Mihaly Csikszentmihalyi, 'Why We Need Things' in Stephen Lubar and David W. Kingery (eds), *History from Things: Essays on Material Culture* (Smithsonian, 1993).

on Princess Street where I kept my record collection. My life was full of adventure at this time, but it was also chaotic, and my living arrangements weren't always ideal.

For a few months I lived with my friends Tina and Debbie above a curry house in Rusholme. My collection was in town, so the girls were in charge of the music. Tina was obsessed with the Princess song 'Say I'm Your Number One'.

I'd started DJ'ing by this point, at small clubs like the Man Alive and the Venue. I'd go first to the office and pick sixty or seventy records, pop them into a cardboard box with a handful of 7" singles, including 'Flesh of My Flesh' by Orange Juice and 'These Boots Are Made For Walkin'' by Nancy Sinatra, and set off for work.

When I bought my first house, in Withington, I had somewhere at last to store and keep all my vinyl close to me. The records were like an army that had marched for miles for years; the survivors were glad to be finally somewhere permanent.

+

DJ Guy Stevens was a rhythm and blues enthusiast in the early 1960s. He'd seek out tunes on black-owned independent record labels that never made it beyond the ghettoised world of race records, and the music that inspired the cover versions and commercial hits.

All week he would trawl for records in specialist record importers like Transat in Soho. He obtained dozens of records via mail order from shops in Louisiana and Tennessee. All the while, he was living in what he later described as a 'one-room, no-water flat' in Leicester Square. Collecting tunes meant everything to him; he was, as the James Brown lyric has it, 'Givin' up food for funk'.

Aficionados would attend his disc-only sessions at the Scene club in Soho, where, every Monday, Guy played rare tunes, music you couldn't hear anywhere else. Regulars included many people who would later make their mark on music; Eric Clapton, Steve Marriott, and Gary Brooker were there, absorbing the sounds, and being inspired by them.

In the history of British rock music, no collection has been a bigger influence or inspiration than the one owned by Guy Stevens.[8] One young man, Pete Meaden, took to hanging out at Guy's flat. After he'd become manager of the Who, Meaden reinvented the band to attract a mod following. He introduced them

[8] More on Guy Stevens in Chapter 3 of my *Adventures on the Wheels of Steel: The Rise of the Superstar DJs* (Fourth Estate, 2001).

to songs like Slim Harpo's 'Got Love If You Want It' and 'I Gotta Dance To Keep From Crying' by the Miracles (the former was the model for 'I'm the Face'; the latter, the Who incorporated into live sets). In addition, it was Guy Stevens playing 'Time Is on My Side' by Irma Thomas that inspired the Rolling Stones to cover the song on their second album.

Records have been the tools of the trade of DJs for decades, of course. If DJs are also remixers and producers, as they so often are, the collection becomes a resource, full of inspiration, and samples.

A bond between a DJ and their record collection is particularly strong. Andrea Kennedy has over ten thousand pieces of vinyl. She is deeply dedicated to the cause of searching for tunes: 'I've missed trains for records. I've taken a walk around the block, found a record shop, and the train and the people I was visiting had to wait. The tunes are my treasures.'

Andrea is one of many female DJs I know, but the gender split among DJs is weighted heavily towards men. This seems to hold true too among vinyl buyers. Emma Pettit writes about independent record shops in her book *Old Rare New*. She confesses one observation is unavoidable: that record stores appear to be 'Male territory. More specifically, male, middle-aged, and white.'⁹

On her travels Emma Pettit meets a host of obsessive and knowledgeable female vinyl collectors, but they are far fewer in number than men, and – as in other areas of the music business (and in so many other areas of life) – seem to have to fight that bit harder to claim respect, and their space.

I know dozens of women with significant record collections, including Kerry Moriarty, who once owned everything on the New York No Wave label Ze Records, and still has substantial collections of certain artists, including Scritti Politti, and Material; Samantha Steele who runs a vinyl record subscription club; and Angela Collings who runs a stall selling vinyl every Saturday and Tuesday at Aylesbury market, every Wednesday in Chesham, and every second and fourth Thursday in Banbury.

Andrea Kennedy made her mark playing venues in Cork like Sir Henry's and Cork Opera House, and Ri-Ra and the Globe in Dublin. She's now based in Poland, has recently DJ'd at several Pride events in Warsaw and Poznan, and has a residency at Kontener Art, an arts space built with and around old shipping containers.

---

[9] Emma Pettit, *Old Rare New: The Independent Record Shop* (Black Dog Publishing, 2008).

When she moved to Poland in 2008 she didn't take her records, DJ'd without them for seven years but was then reunited with her collection. She worked at a pirate radio station with her boyfriend, having merged their record collections. They broke up and the only way she could be certain her tunes were safe was to ship them all to Poland. She keeps around a thousand records with her – what she thinks of as her working collection. The rest are in a lockup (it's not unusual for DJs to have collections at different locations; Pete Tong has his records in three different places across two continents).

How you organise and store a record collection is almost as important and as personal as the contents.[10] This is one of the biggest distinctions between collecting and the related activity of hoarding: collectors are in control. In addition, hoarders seldom derive any pleasure from accruing items; they've lost a battle against chaos.

My collection was neatly shelved, although my records were never listed, or catalogued in any way. I stored them in a primitive, perhaps slightly chaotic system, but I knew where every record could

---

[10] There's a new guidebook by Philippe Blanchet and Frederic Beghin called *L'art de ranger ses disques* (Rivages Rouge, 2019), explaining how to organise a vinyl collection.

be found. Roughly. Usually.

The records were kept in a walk-in record store in the cellar of my house in south Manchester. The cellar included two rooms and a smaller room where my collection was housed on floor-to-ceiling shelving. My turntables were in one of the other rooms, along with around a thousand records; they were usually the ones I'd then be playing most often in clubs, the ones I'd need closest to hand.

The main method, if you can call it a 'method', was to store the records by the label they were released on, but only if the label was important to me and the collection: labels such as Factory, Def Jam, Talkin' Loud, Warp, and R&S were well represented. I had a sizeable collection of Italo House, music from labels like UMM, Media, Irma, and Palmares.

If the record wasn't released by one of my most-favoured labels, then it went into a section with other miscellaneous records of a similar kind or genre – be-bop, 1960s rock, New York house, and a genre that I thought of as 'things that sounded a bit like Cabaret Voltaire'.

DJ'ing, I was also the recipient of a few free records each week, from labels like Champion, Strictly Rhythm and Boy's Own. In addition to DJ'ing, I'd spent some years writing in fanzines and music papers and magazines; Rough Trade and Factory Records sent me a lot of stuff when I had a fanzine. Among the white labels in my collection, there were records by Sonic Youth, New Order, and Primal Scream, and an unplayed, limited-edition Aphex Twin remix of a St Etienne single with a value around £70. I had a copy of *The Frenz Experiment* by the Fall defaced by Mark E Smith. The rarest records included God Within's 'Raincry' on white vinyl which sells for £90.

I never bought a record as an investment or to sell on. The only times I traded records were when I was sent something which I had no use for. When that happened, I'd take a trip to Vinyl Exchange and hope they'd take some ludicrous Martin Garrix remix of Christina Aguilera's 'Your Body' off me for cash instead of it going straight into the bin.

I was being sent records but I would still purchase a lot too. From 1986 I was DJ'ing two nights a week at the Haçienda. All of us in the residents team instinctively understood that we should be aiming to be different, eclectic, and new. My search for tunes would include looking for things no one else was playing, leftfield stuff, underground tunes. In the mid 1980s, the biggest influence on what I bought and played was not magazines or other club DJs, but a radio DJ called Steve Barker who presented a show on BBC Radio Lancashire. He introduced me to the On U Sound label, for example; their releases became key to helping me build a reputation in Manchester's clubs.

At the end of the 1980s, though, most tunes I added to my collection were tracks I first heard in record stores. I'd always had a good relationship with the staff at Piccadilly Records. If I was paying for an early Pastels release or something, they'd grab some record that had just come in and ask, 'If you like that, have you tried this?'

Eastern Bloc started out as a stall in Affleck's Palace called Earwig. The staff would often recommend tunes to me; I remember buying Cold Cut's semi-official release 'Beats & Pieces' from there in the mid 1980s, and records like Sweet Tee and Jazzy Joyce's 'It's My Beat'. I must have bought almost everything they ever stocked on labels like Profile, Sleeping Bag, and Def Jam.

Sometimes I would go to Spin Inn too, and, in the 1990s, Manchester Underground. Record shops are integral to the story of Manchester as a successful music city – believing in the music, sourcing the tunes, and giving us access to them.

My visits to Eastern Bloc in the early 1990s increased to at least twice weekly. The deeper I got into

DJ'ing, the more my collection reflected that. When I came to sell my records, two-thirds of the 4,500 tunes were records I'd played at clubs between 1987 and 1998 – clubs like the Haçienda, the Boardwalk, and Sankeys in Manchester, Angels in Burnley, and Cream in Liverpool – and taken with me abroad, to Paris, Berlin, the USA.

I've fallen in love with a lot of music. I dragged the records from club to club and country to country, played them in dark, chaotic venues, dropped them, sometimes lost them. They got drenched in beer, and exposed to mess and chaos. I knew I couldn't sell them to any online buyer or to a dealer looking for records that could be classified as being in 'good' condition, or 'good +', let alone 'mint'. I'd have to make up a new category called 'wrong sleeves, dusty'.

+

I met Daniel Soutif through a friend of a friend on one of my visits to Paris in the months following the sale of my records. His record collection takes my breath away.

Daniel lives four or five hundred yards from the Place de la Bastille, overlooking a quiet courtyard behind a busy street full of bars. Walking into his very neat rooms, I didn't know where to start; in addition to rows and rows of vinyl, the rooms were also full of art history books and 1940s music magazines.

Perching myself on a sofa, I wasn't sure I was ever going to be able to drag myself away from his company or his collection. My first question was: 'Can I live here?' The sofa seemed very comfortable. I decided I'd be fine to bed down there, and with occasional injections of coffee I'd be very happy.

Daniel's interest in jazz started as a teenager in the 1950s when he became a regular listener to a weekday radio show entitled 'Pour ceux qui aiment le jazz' ('for those who like jazz'). Presenters Frank Ténot and Daniel Filipacchi played mostly new records released in the United States. 'It was each evening at ten past ten, and they were broadcasting for almost one hour,' Daniel recalls. 'It was a lucky moment, it was just before sleep and you had done your homework, and the two guys presenting were very informed.'

There was a thriving local jazz scene, but jazz was very much a minority interest, says Daniel. 'At school we were a few who had this interest, a kind of elite you might say. Just a few of us had this common interest, maybe 10 per cent of the people.'

Daniel and the other listeners were jazz aficionados, the true believers. The show used to begin with 'Blue March' by Art Blakey & the Jazz Messengers, broadcast live concerts most Wednesdays, and show-cased new releases on Fridays. Many of the records played on the show you couldn't find in Paris. The best chance of finding the latest jazz was at a shop near Galeries Lafayette called Les Disques du Monde Entier ('the records of all the world').

Another obstacle to owning music was lack of money. Daniel remembers going record-shopping with his sister. It was almost exactly sixty years ago, when they went to Les Disques du Monde Entier with only enough francs for either *Kind of Blue* by Miles Davis or an album by a Belgian sax player called Bobby Jaspar and the French vibraphone player Michel Hausser which was released around the same time.

Daniel had read of *Kind of Blue* in the French jazz magazines, he knew it was an important record, but his sister wanted to buy the Bobby Jaspar record. 'We had the money for one LP,' he says. 'And after a heavy discussion we bought the Miles Davis.'

Kind of Blue has so much significance, he doesn't regret the purchase; but he tells me that from a collector's point of view, it was the wrong choice. '*Kind of Blue* never became rare but the Bobby Jaspar became very rare. Occasionally I have seen that record on sale for something like a thousand dollars.'

In the early 1960s, Daniel began taking an interest in classical music. He was – and still is – fascinated by Bach, but he had a particular enthusiasm for contemporary, avant-garde classical music too. Albums released by Phillips in an advanced, challenging collection called Modern Music Series featured reproductions of abstract paintings on the front of the record sleeves. Daniel wants to show me a Modern Music Series release – a collection of works by Webern.

'Don't get up,' he says to me. He's in his mid seventies so he is a little creaky, but I let him go find the record.

'Somewhere I have the complete set where it was coming from,' he says. 'Let me see…'

He stretches up. I don't think he can reach it.

'I don't know where I put it,' he says.

I am a little surprised he can't put his hand on it immediately; I thought there would be a system, all the albums would be categorised and easy to find.

'Maybe it is a little bit higher,' he says, and then he spots it, more or less where he thought it was, far right on the top shelf. He grabs a chair.

At this point, I do actually stand up; I have visions he's going to break his neck looking for a rare Webern.

'Ah, you are sufficiently high,' he says, as I go to help him. I don't need a chair, I reach up.

'Yes, just there, *oui*, the first one.'

We have the record, and return to our coffees. He holds the sleeve, turns it over. 'I was fascinated by Webern,' he tells me.

Was the look of the sleeve part of the attraction?

'Oh yes, it was perfect.'

It was an era when many releases featured amazing designs. People like Reid Miles were producing fantastic sleeve artwork for the Blue Note label. Columbia Records employed S. Neil Fujita; his sleeve for the 1959 Charles Mingus album *Mingus Ah Um* is glorious.

Their aesthetic appealed to Daniel: the complete, physical, cherishable, artistic package. Images and concert footage weren't accessible, so sleeves functioned also as clues towards a more fully three-dimensional sense of the music and the artist. Sleeve notes even more so; the sleeve notes to *Mingus Ah Um* featured words penned by Diane Dorr-Dorynek.

Daniel tried to explain why the combination of jazz and avant-garde visuals made such a huge impression on him. His father was a factory worker, his mother worked in a supermarket. 'We were very poor, my father was working all day long in a factory, and in the evening he did work for cash. He died very young.'

He holds the Webern record. 'I think this music and records like this, the cover, the beauty of it, it was symbolically also something; these records were signs of another kind of society probably.'

The class struggle was intense, the Algerian war was ongoing. 'It was a heavy situation,' says Daniel.

The record implied or suggested the possibility of another world?

'Yes, I think, but I didn't consider this at the time, but looking back I can see that aspect to my interest.'

He was intrigued by the world of ideas and studied philosophy at university, later becoming a philosophy lecturer, an art critic, an exhibition curator, and a contributor to the Paris-based *Jazz Magazine*. He always found the time to frequent record shops, buying vintage jazz records from the 1920s – including some with the very first picture sleeves – and he chased down new releases too.

Access to the music in the 1970s improved; there were shops selling old and new jazz records everywhere, throughout *le monde entier*. When Daniel was in London he'd make his way to Dobells on Charing Cross Road. He had his regular record haunts in Amsterdam, and in Brussels: 'A strange guy had a shop on the periphery of Brussels who considered you stupid. You ask for a record, any record, and he treated you like some kind of shit.'

He sees little difference between the hours spent in record shops browsing for records and the hours he now spends on the internet. 'I am fascinated by the way I can still discover musicians.'

There are endless, unresolvable discussions to be had regarding whether the quality of music has deteriorated in the last thirty, forty, fifty years, and clearly the ways we consume recorded music have changed, but it's worth noting that hunger for music is still strong. Album sales might be falling, but according to the BPI there were approximately 91 billion audio streams in 2018[11] – the equivalent of the UK's 27 million households each listening to 3,370 songs over the course of the year.

Daniel is enthused by how he can track music on the internet – new music, but also old music that he was previously unaware of. He recently discovered the existence in the 1960s of a quintet led by Don

[11] Figures announced January 2019 and detailed on the BPI website, https://www.bpi.co.uk/news-analysis/music-movie-boost-helps-british-music-consumption-rise-again-in-2018 (consulted January 2019).

Rendell and Ian Carr. He's started listening to albums the quintet recorded between 1965 and 1979: 'They are magnificent. Then I started listening to things connected. For example, the piano player in the quintet, Michael Garrick, recorded music at the same time, which is interesting also.'

There are several vinyl stores currently thriving in Paris, including Walrus, Balades Sonores and Betino's. Daniel mentions Paris Jazz Corner on Rue de Navarre. 'Maybe you should go there,' he says. 'You may see a lot of crazy people there.'

I assume he means obsessed collectors. I hesitate, wondering if my next question is going to cause offence. 'But, can I ask you, though, are you one of the crazy people?'

'Oh yes, I think! I consider I am crazy, yes, and I spend a lot of time thinking of such questions!' He's a French philosopher; of course he does.

'But you know there are different kinds of crazy people,' he goes on, smiling. 'To me the craziness finds its justification in the way I told you about Don Rendell and Ian Carr. For weeks you listen to things you know well, and then one day you discover something that you don't know, and that is really fantastic…'

We're obsessed, they're obsessed…

'They're obsessed, yes. They want something which is rare, which for them is the most important reason, maybe the only reason. They have heard of blues records with two copies in existence and maybe they want both.'

Owning something rare gives them pleasure but also power perhaps? And money too; you can sell the rarity to make some.

'Yes, there are different people in the world; some people want power or money and some people want something else. I want something else.'

Something intangible?

He doesn't answer directly. 'I guess some people who consider themselves serious collectors are not really interested in the music, they like the collecting, and the records, but I don't feel from them a real taste for the music. I'm not this kind. The basic aspect of my craziness is for the music itself.'

Nevertheless, one of the features of Daniel's collection – not just the vinyl, but also the metres and metres of shelving containing art books, jazz books, magazines, videos, albums, singles, cassettes, box sets – is that it's a wonderful archive. The collection tells important stories beyond Daniel's personal history; about culture, art, and Black American creativity, for example. Some of the items in his collection featured in a 2009 exhibition he curated at Musée du Quai Branly called *Le Siècle du Jazz*, demonstrating the ways jazz reflected and shaped painting, photography, design, film, literature, and politics through the twentieth century.[12]

In some ways he is operating like a museum or a library or some cultural institution might, saving items for posterity, for analysis, for ever. 'I do consider that these things shouldn't disappear, yes,' he tells me.

I was wondering what would happen if he wanted to move house. There's so much stuff gathered in his home, it would be a major deal to move. What he said next was maybe a little morbid but also funny. 'We cannot move from here. We can only die here.'

+

My father is fifteen years older than Daniel, in his late eighties. Recently, he's had his share of illnesses. A few years back he collapsed at home, his pulse disappeared, but the ambulance service saved him and the NHS nursed him back to reasonable health.

Since that moment he's started to consider what he might leave behind. He's kept stuff, with-

---

[12] Daniel also curated a related exhibition at Musée du Quai Branly in 2016 called *The Color Line*, showcasing the work of African-American artists during the segregation era.

out ever thinking of himself as a collector. What he's amassed reflects his interests, and various phases in his life; including railway magazines, Ordnance Survey maps, and guides to cathedrals, mostly neatly stored in folders and boxes.

You don't have to consider yourself to have much of a collecting impulse to hang on to things. Inevitably, some of all our accumulated stuff will be parcelled into boxes at our passing. You know, also, some will go into a skip. The number of boxes of stuff we leave behind may amount to fifty, or maybe thirty-five. Or maybe only one: pictures your kids drew when they were little, love letters your grandparents exchanged between the wars, some postcards, your favourite mug, an out-of-date passport.

What happens when we go? The items that we leave behind may have some monetary value, but when what's in the boxes loses its owner, it maybe loses its meaning too. It's only our own life and personality that explains the logic behind what we've collected.

Maybe an ending comes sooner than we expect, or a certain type of ending. For example, I wonder what a collector does when a lifelong chase ends, a set is completed, and there are no more Ze Records releases to collect?

I asked Dec Hickey if and when he gets to the

point when every José Feliciano want is fulfilled, the chase is over, and the collection is complete, how will he feel? 'I don't know,' he says. 'Does a light go out somewhere in the brain?'

A collection is a life's work, you'll want to know what will go where, who gets what. One aspect of collecting – certainly cataloguing – is to exert control over the general chaos of life. A collector will hope to be in control even at, and beyond, the end, as opposed to facing the trauma of having a collection destroyed, or stolen.

While he was serving time in prison after a drugs bust, Guy Stevens's record collection was stolen from his mother's house. In the months afterwards, he discovered the thief had sold all the records at the equivalent of 3p or 4p each. The collection had been scattered to the four winds. Guy later reflected on the trauma: 'The guy didn't know what he was selling. I had every Miracles record. Every Muddy Waters record. I had every Chess record from 001...'

Guy's personal problems were piling up – he'd had some bad luck in his work in the music industry, and his drug use and prison sentence sapped his morale – but it was the loss of his record collection which appears to have been the event that triggered a breakdown. He'd lost the tools of his trade, his inspiration, his life's work and even, I guess, his identity. He subsequently had some success in the music business but was always haunted by his loss.

Daniel is unsure what he might be able to plan for the future of his vinyl collection. He tells me how a friend of his had died and some of his collection disappeared, and other bits were sold off, dispersed. It's clearly important to collectors that a collection isn't broken up.

Will Keith ever part with his trainer collection, or will Claudia Schiffer say goodbye to her insects? For some people, their collecting days end under pressure from major life issues, for example, or lack of money, or just running out of space. Space wasn't really a problem for me; there would have been room for more shelving and more tunes in the cellar if I'd wanted to extend my vinyl collection.

So why did I decide to sell my records?

I'd stopped using vinyl at my DJ gigs after a couple of incidents. One was a booking at Bowlers, a multi-room Manchester venue. The technical guys had most things covered but unfortunately no knowledge of how to set up decks on a stage; the records jumped and skidded, and my set was abandoned. With eight hundred people there.

Instead of using vinyl, I'd been burning CDs

of tracks, most of which I'd downloaded, and many unavailable on vinyl. This was another thing: if I'd stuck to vinyl only, I'd have denied myself the pleasure of playing many of the best tunes I was listening to and wanted to share.

When Guy Stevens lost his collection, he'd probably lost the chance of hearing many of his records ever again. But 99 per cent of my favourite music is just a click of a mouse away for me. I was saying goodbye to the vinyl but not the music.

I knew I didn't need the records in any practical sense, but the idea of selling them all was sudden and instinctive. I knew what they represented – their personal, musical, archival, and even financial value to me – but what slightly surprised me was that I had lost enough emotional attachment to them to let go.

Maybe there were some deep reasons for this. In her poem 'The Journey', Mary Oliver hears an insistent inner voice crying to her: 'Mend my life!' It was like that. I guess it was partly the result of a midlife wobble, some of it connected to family, and my work. My kids were on great form, but my marriage had hit a difficult phase. I felt isolated, I was struggling to sparkle, and had a couple of panic attacks and increasing insomnia; the doctor diagnosed reactive depression.

My DJ work was still giving me joy on most

occasions and on many levels, but the relentless messing with my body clock was savage. But it was also hard to deal with the battering my psyche was getting. During a DJ gig, you feel very loved by the people in the room; it's temporary, and an illusion, of course, but it's hard to tell your psyche that. You wake up, it's over, and the rush has gone. You'd think it's likely you'd get accustomed to this comedown, but I haven't.

In addition to the post-event hollowness, or post-event blues, or whatever it is, I also began to understand that I was going through a hangover on a bigger scale. As you get older, it's tempting to feel your best days are over, and to feel opportunities are diminishing. I was lucky to have participated in a wonderful music scene at the Haçienda in the 1980s – a scene that is probably more famous now than it was then. I love the idea of celebrating it and I understood in many ways it defined me but, at the same time, I didn't want it to rule me for the rest of my life.

I remember words Neneh Cherry used when I interviewed her and we talked about her looking back at her younger self, her *Top of the Pops* debut nearly three decades earlier, her hit single with 'Buffalo Stance'. 'It's all a part of where I am now,' she told me. 'It's why I am where I am now. But you have to allow yourself to move on.'

I was past the age that my mother was when she died – she was 52. Was I running out of time? I was full of self-doubt, and not sure I knew exactly what I wanted my future to look like or even what futures were available, but I felt the need to break the continuum, to challenge myself, and to embrace the recklessness of the moment. When you feel forced to mend your life, and find yourself in a deeply emotional, but chaotic and vulnerable, moment, then you do consider all options. Should I tinker with things, or maybe give my life something more of a jolt? Selling my records was one of the biggest decisions I could take.

My son and my daughter were both perplexed. Their earliest memories include me dragging record boxes out of the front door and into a taxi and leaving for work. My son asked me why I didn't pick out a few records that meant something to me before selling them. I took two out, randomly, sentimentally, as keepsakes for the kids: my daughter ended up with a Blondie 12" single. 'If I started going through the rest one by one and wondering if I could justify keeping them, I'd keep them all,' I explained. 'They all mean something.'

Somehow, though, the records had also come to represent the baggage of my past and I needed to lighten the load. Of course, my past isn't bad – a lot of it is fantastic – but it was weighing heavy on me. Being stuck in the past – allowing too much nostalgia into your life – holds you back and destroys your creativity. I needed to move on. I was going to sell my past to help create my future.

I am unsure I have a handle on the complete explanation, though. Things can be confused and blurred in life. You can drift apart from someone and never quite work out why, and make decisions it's impossible to map out reasons for, or reduce to bullet points. As writer Maggie Nelson puts it in her memoir, *The Argonauts*: 'How to explain, in a culture frantic for resolution, that sometimes the shit stays messy?'[13]

+

I posted a picture of my collection on Facebook, explained the whole lot was for sale and awaited responses. The story was picked up on multiple music websites, my inboxes went bonkers.

The collection was erratic and eclectic, but that was part of its charm. It certainly contained enough evidence to nail the lie of the sixties generation that the best days in music, culture, and excitement

---

[13] Maggie Nelson, *The Argonauts* (Graywolf Press, 2015).

were over before the 1970s. Also, to some potential buyers, my connections to the Haçienda gave the collection some added interest and value. To come up with a price, a record dealer estimated the retail value of the collection, and then I added 25 per cent. As I said to him, 'Some of these records might be covered in dust, but it's Haçienda dust.'

I got two serious offers, both from people happy to pay the asking price. An art collector in Italy, Mauro Del Rio, had some intriguing ideas about exhibiting the collection in a converted church in Parma, and placing it at the centre of an event programme. The other offer was from Seth Troxler, whose delightful first email to me began: 'Hello Dave, my name is Seth Troxler. I'm currently one of the biggest DJs in the world...'

We can look backwards endlessly, nostalgically, or the past – our past – can be inspiration and ammunition for the future. I liked Seth's suggestion that he would take the records with him on his DJ travels; my record collection could live on, but now as part of Seth's story. The records could sit in my cellar for ever, but instead I was setting the music free. Saying goodbye to my records was like saying goodbye to a gang of friends leaving town for a new life on the other side of the world.

In some ways, the letting-go was also exhilarating. I realised I wasn't just surviving selling my record collection; I was surviving *by* selling my record collection.

The extra cash I got from selling the collection I spent on an extended stay in Paris. I'd always wanted to live there. In part it was a breathing space, but in other ways it was a challenge; to live there alone, with no props, no plan, and a limited knowledge of the language.

I hadn't rid myself of my hundreds of books, or the boxes of letters and postcards and nightlife memorabilia I've accrued and saved, but letting go of the record collection did make me feel lighter. I had moments of Zen-like calmness; I began to think there was some merit in resisting the tyranny of stuff; I wondered whether we own possessions or they own us; and I am still not convinced that if you want something intangible, you're going to get that by amassing tangible things.

In the aftermath of the sale, I became friends with Seth. He came up to Manchester to see a New Order show that I'd helped to organise and then we DJ'd together at an event which raised £4,000 for mental health charities. Occasionally, still, he'll message me if he's been digging into my collection and found something new to him which he's enjoyed hearing.

Even though Mauro missed out on acquiring the collection, we've since worked together on several projects. Most recently, I helped arrange a week of events at his old church in Parma, took the band LIINES over, performed an ambient soundscape called 'Breathless' which is built around the sound of my heartbeat. And threw a party...

I still love the chance to browse through other people's records. I love and appreciate vinyl as much as ever. I'm finding it impossible to walk past a vinyl store and not have just a little root around, but so far I am just about managing to resist buying records and building a new collection from scratch. To help deter myself from doing so, I got the turntables out of my house – and lent them to my son, Jack.

Jack used to think my record collection would be part of his inheritance, and that I'd deprived him of that joy. But ultimately every generation makes its own culture, every person makes their own life and their own choices; every person has to jump barriers and find passions of their own. Even before I lent him turntables he was into music. I always believed that one day he would build his own record collection. And he has.

ORIGINAL ILLUSTRATION, DESIGN & TYPESETTING

Zoë McLean, Manchester
zoe@confingopublishing.uk

BODY TYPE

Minion 3, an updated and expanded version of
Robert Slimbach's early 90s design for Adobe.

COVER TYPE

Futura PT, developed at ParaType in 1995 by Vladimir
Yefimov, expands on the classic geometric sans-serif type-
face Futura designed by Paul Renner in 1927.

OTHER BOOKS BY CŌNFINGŌ PUBLISHING

Ornithology: Sixteen Short Stories Nicholas Royle

We Were Strangers: Stories Inspired by Unknown Pleasures
(ed. Richard V. Hirst)

Pharricide Vincent de Swarte (translated by Nicholas Royle)

CŌNFINGŌ

confingopublishing.uk